Sailing
on the
Mayflower

IMAGINE YOU WERE THERE...

Sailing on the Mayflower

CARYN JENNER

KINGFISHER
LONDON & NEW YORK

KINGFISHER
LONDON & NEW YORK

I had nearly finished writing this book, when I discovered I have a family link to the Mayflower Pilgrims, through distant cousins! —Caryn Jenner

Distributed in the U.S. and Canada by Macmillan, 120 Broadway, New York, NY 10271
Library of Congress Cataloging-in-Publication data has been applied for.

Series editor: Elizabeth Yeates
Illustrations: Marc Pattenden (Advocate Art Agency)
Design: Dan Newman
Cover design: Laura Hall

ISBN: 978-0-7534-7529-4

Kingfisher books are available for special promotions and premiums. For details contact: Special Markets Department, Macmillan, 120 Broadway, New York, NY 10271.

For more information, please visit:
www.kingfisherbooks.com

Printed in China

9 8 7 6 5 4 3 2 1
1TR/0819/WKT/UG/128MA

Contents

The Pilgrims' Adventure

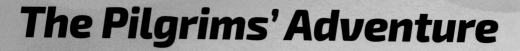

Imagine moving away from your home and sailing across the ocean to a new land. The voyage is dangerous, and you're not sure what you'll find when you arrive. You're excited, but scared, too. Will you arrive safely? Where will you live when you arrive?

Throughout history, people have moved around to different places. Sometimes people move nearby, to a place that might already be familiar. Sometimes they make new homes all the way on the other side of the world.

Pilgrims

A pilgrim is any person who makes a journey, especially a religious journey. The people who founded the colony of Plymouth are known as the Pilgrims.

In 1620, one group of people set sail from Europe on a ship called the *Mayflower*. They crossed the Atlantic Ocean to make their new home in the largely unknown land of North America, where they founded the settlement of Plymouth in Massachusetts. They became known as the Pilgrims. This is their story.

⇦ *More than 100 passengers boarded the Mayflower and set sail for the New World.*

Religion in England

Who were the Pilgrims, and why did they want to move to a new home? Many of the Pilgrims were part of a religious group called Separatists, who in turn were a branch of the Puritans. They wanted to move so they could worship freely, something they were not allowed to do in England. The problems had started about a century before.

King Henry VIII:
"The Kings of England in times past never had any superior but God."

King Henry VIII (reigned 1509—1547)

In 1534, Henry founded the Church of England when the Catholic pope in Rome refused him permission to divorce his wife, Catherine of Aragon (the first of his six wives). The Church of England was a new form of Protestant Christianity that became the country's official religion, with King Henry as its supreme head.

⇧ Catherine of Aragon was Henry VIII's first wife.

Queen Elizabeth I
(reigned 1558—1603)

Elizabeth's reign is sometimes considered a golden age in English history. That's when William Shakespeare started writing and performing his famous plays, and explorers such as Walter Raleigh and Francis Drake claimed new lands for the queen. Many of the Pilgrims grew up with Elizabeth on the throne.

Queen Elizabeth I: "There is one thing higher than royalty, and that is religion."

King James I: "I will make them conform themselves or else I will harry them out of this land, or else do worse."

King James I
(reigned 1603—1625)

James was a harsh king who was intolerant of religions other than the Church of England. Puritans wanted to change the Church, but King James refused to tolerate them.

Some Puritans decided that in order to worship in the way they believed, they had to separate themselves from the Church of England. They were known as Separatists.

9

Young William Bradford

William Bradford was born in 1590 in Austerfield, Yorkshire, in England. His parents died when he was a child, so he lived with relatives. William was a lonely, sickly boy. When he was about 12 years old, he began studying the Bible.

Young William decided that he didn't agree with the Church of England. He joined Separatist Puritans, who worshipped in secret at the home of William Brewster, in the nearby town of Scrooby.

The Separatists' beliefs chimed with William's. At last, he felt that he belonged. William Bradford soon became a dedicated member of the congregation, and William Brewster became his adviser.

William Brewster:
"We follow the rules laid out in the Bible for running our church."

Governor Bradford

William Bradford grew up to become governor of the Pilgrims' settlement in Plymouth. Most of the information that we have about the Mayflower voyage and the settlement in Plymouth comes from his memoir, Of Plymouth Plantation.

⇦ *William Brewster was a leading member of the congregation, which would gather on his farm.*

Escape from England

Twice the Separatists planned their escape from England to Holland so they could worship freely.

The first time, the ship's captain double-crossed them and notified royal officals, who arrested the Separatist leaders. They were in prison for several months.

The second time, royal officials showed up while the Separatists were loading the ship. The captain set sail to Holland with some men on board but left the women and children behind in England.

⇩ Separatist leaders were arrested and put in jail because they wanted to leave England, which was not allowed.

Eventually, the Separatists were all reunited in the Dutch capital of Amsterdam. They lived there for a year and then moved to the Dutch city of Leiden. But it wasn't the home they had dreamed of. The Separatists wanted to create a brand-new community, where they could live and worship as they wanted. They decided that the answer lay across the ocean in the New World.

William Bradford

While in Leiden, William Bradford married Dorothy May and they had a son, John. He wrote of the decision to head to the New World: "It was granted that the dangers were great . . . the difficulties were many, but not invincible."

The Separatists, including the children, worked long hours making cloth, which didn't leave much time for worship. The adults feared that the children would lose their religion.

The New World

The New World refers to the continents of North and South America and the Caribbean Islands. For thousands of years, it was home to Native Americans, whose tribes were spread around the land.

By the time of the Pilgrims' *Mayflower* voyage in 1620, sailors from Europe and around the globe had been exploring the New World for over a century.

The Pilgrims must have heard about these explorations to the New World and decided that it was a good place for their new settlement.

Jamestown, Virginia

In 1607, Captain John Smith led the creation of a settlement in Jamestown, Virginia. A Native American girl named Pocahontas befriended John Smith and the settlers, and it's largely thanks to her that Jamestown survived.

Jamestown

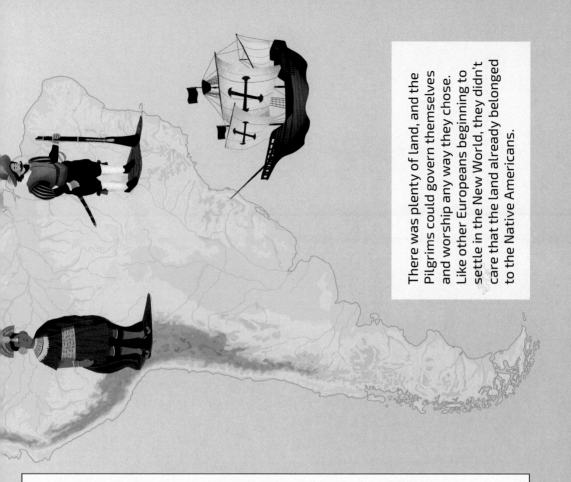

There was plenty of land, and the Pilgrims could govern themselves and worship any way they chose. Like other Europeans beginning to settle in the New World, they didn't care that the land already belonged to the Native Americans.

New World explorations

There were explorations of the New World before 1620, which is when the Pilgrims set sail on the Mayflower.

Christopher Columbus sailed to the Caribbean from Spain in 1492. He is often given credit as the first to cross the ocean to explore the New World, but no one knows for sure.

Italian explorer Amerigo Vespucci sailed to the Americas in the early 1500s. America is named after him.

Francisco Pizarro and his 167 soldiers arrived in South America looking for gold in 1532.

From 1534, Jacques Cartier made three trips to the New World. He gave Canada its name.

Spanish explorer Hernando de Soto discovered the Mississippi River in 1541.

Samuel de Champlain founded the city of Quebec in 1608. People in Quebec still speak both French and English.

In the 1600s, Henry Hudson set off to find China, but landed in the New World and explored the Hudson River.

Saying Farewell

The Pilgrims' voyage to the New World took three years to organize. The Separatists needed official permission to set up a colony in America. They also needed money.

John Carver and Robert Cushman arranged for a group of investors called "merchant adventurers" to pay for the voyage to America. The Separatists promised to pay back the investors once they were settled. They would establish their colony near the mouth of the Hudson River on the northeast coast.

⇧ *Gold and silver coins from the early 17th century.*

Reluctantly, they also agreed for other passengers to join them on the voyage. The Separatists called these other passengers "Strangers" because they didn't know them until they met on the voyage. Although Carver and Cushman didn't trust Thomas Weston, who represented the merchant adventurers, they felt that they had to agree to the terms offered. Otherwise, how would they get to America?

⇩ *Robert Weir painted* Embarkation of the Pilgrims, *which shows the Pilgrims on board the* Speedwell.

On July 22, 1620, around 125 Separatists set sail from Holland on a ship called the *Speedwell*. The departure was met with excitement and fear about the adventure and dangers that lay ahead. There was also sadness, because many families were split up, with some members going to America while others stayed behind.

⇩ Family members may have watched as the Speedwell *departed.*

William Bradford: "The wind being fair, they went aboard, and their friends with them, where truly doleful was the sight of that sad and mournful parting."

17

Setting Sail

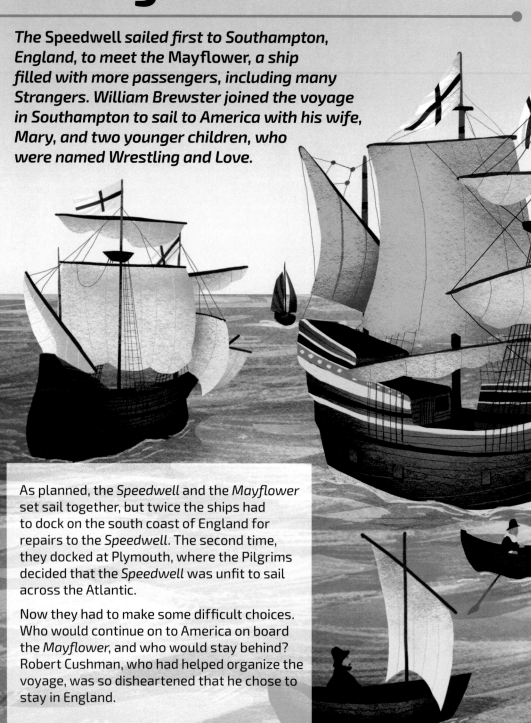

The Speedwell *sailed first to Southampton, England, to meet the* Mayflower, *a ship filled with more passengers, including many Strangers. William Brewster joined the voyage in Southampton to sail to America with his wife, Mary, and two younger children, who were named Wrestling and Love.*

As planned, the *Speedwell* and the *Mayflower* set sail together, but twice the ships had to dock on the south coast of England for repairs to the *Speedwell*. The second time, they docked at Plymouth, where the Pilgrims decided that the *Speedwell* was unfit to sail across the Atlantic.

Now they had to make some difficult choices. Who would continue on to America on board the *Mayflower*, and who would stay behind? Robert Cushman, who had helped organize the voyage, was so disheartened that he chose to stay in England.

On September 6, 1620, the *Mayflower* finally set sail from Plymouth, with 102 impatient passengers on board. They'd already used up some of their provisions during the frustrating delays. What's more, summer was now turning into fall, which meant winter was fast approaching. The Pilgrims needed to get to America as soon as possible.

The *Speedwell*

The Pilgrims suspected that the captain of the Speedwell *had tricked them. The* Speedwell *was later sold and refitted, and went on to make many profitable voyages.*

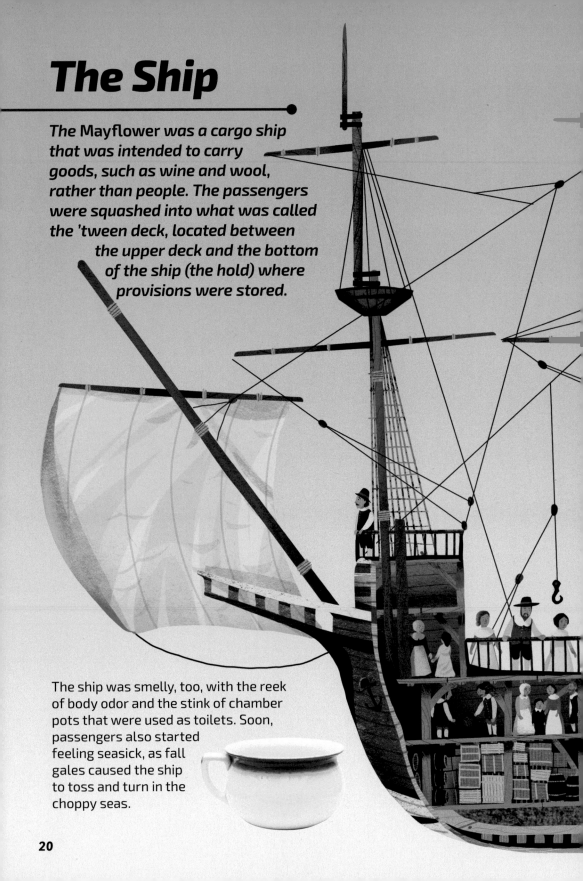

The Ship

The Mayflower was a cargo ship that was intended to carry goods, such as wine and wool, rather than people. The passengers were squashed into what was called the 'tween deck, located between the upper deck and the bottom of the ship (the hold) where provisions were stored.

The ship was smelly, too, with the reek of body odor and the stink of chamber pots that were used as toilets. Soon, passengers also started feeling seasick, as fall gales caused the ship to toss and turn in the choppy seas.

⇩ The Mayflower was crammed with people, animals, and cargo.

Navigating the way

The captain, Master Christopher Jones, was an experienced seaman. He used a magnetic compass to help keep the Mayflower on course across the vast Atlantic Ocean. To estimate the ship's speed, he counted the knots on a small, flat piece of wood that was attached to a rope and thrown overboard.

⇧ A compass was used to check that the ship was sailing in the correct direction.

The deck had very low ceilings; adults could not even stand upright. People erected thin walls around the patch of wooden deck that they claimed for themselves and their families. The result was a dark, damp, crowded maze of makeshift rooms packed with people and their precious belongings.

The crew

There were 20–30 crew members working on board. The ship's surgeon, Giles Heale, was kept very busy with sick passengers.

Mayflower Passengers

The 102 passengers on the Mayflower were a varied group of people, who are now known together as Pilgrims. They included families with children, couples, single men, and some servants.

About half of the Pilgrims were Separatists, and half were Strangers. The Separatists and Strangers did not have much in common, and at first they were suspicious of each other. They had different beliefs and different ways of living. They came from different places and spoke differently. Some could read and write, while others could not.

Separatists

Catherine Carver

John Carver

Desire Minter

John Howland

William Bradford

Dorothy Bradford

George Soule

William Brewster

Mary Brewster

Ellen More

Elizabeth Winslow

Edward Winslow

Elias Story

Mary More

Richard More

Wrestling Brewster

Love Brewster

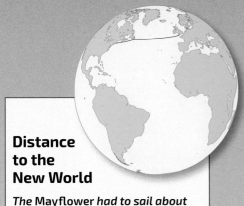

Distance to the New World

The Mayflower had to sail about 2,750 mi. (4,426 km) from Plymouth, England, across the Atlantic Ocean.

What the Separatists and Strangers did have in common was the dream of a bright new future in the New World. They came to realize that it was vital to get along and work together if the venture were to have any chance of success—and the first challenge was the voyage across the Atlantic Ocean.

Strangers

Crew

Christopher Jones (captain)

John Allerton

Myles Standish

Rose Standish

John Clarke (ship's pilot)

Solomon Prower

Mary Martin

Christopher Martin

John Langemore

Giles Heale (ship's surgeon)

Constance Hopkins

Giles Hopkins

John Alden (cooper)

Damaris Hopkins

Elizabeth Hopkins

Stephen Hopkins

Children on the Mayflower

There were about 30 children on the Mayflower, *from babies up to teenagers. In fact, there was even a baby born during the voyage.*

Elizabeth Hopkins was several months pregnant when the *Mayflower* set sail. She named her baby Oceanus. He joined his sisters, Constance and Damaris, and brother, Giles, who were all making the journey. Their father, Stephen Hopkins, was one of the few passengers who had been to America before.

The More children—Ellen, Jasper, Richard, and Mary—were four young sisters and brothers who sailed on the *Mayflower* without their parents. They were looked after by other families.

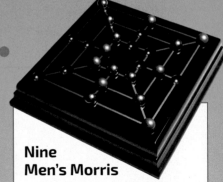

Nine Men's Morris

The children on the Mayflower may have played Nine Men's Morris, a board game that is many hundreds of years old.

⇩ *The older children looked after the younger ones.*

Children on the *Mayflower* had to stay out of the way of the busy sailors. Although they didn't have space to run around, they could still sing, do needlework, and play indoor games on the 'tween deck. The children probably had lessons on board the ship using hornbooks.

The children on the *Mayflower* represented the future. The Pilgrims were very aware that the voyage to America would not only change their lives and the lives of their children, but the New World would become home to their children's children and generations to come.

Hornbook

A hornbook was a wooden board (not a book at all!) with ABCs or other lessons. It was covered by a protective coating of clear horn.

⇩ *Children played games to help pass the time during the long journey.*

A Packed Ship

The Pilgrims had to pack the Mayflower with everything they needed for a voyage to America, plus everything they might need to set up home once they arrived. They didn't expect to ever return to Europe, so they also wanted to bring things that were too precious to leave behind. Most of their personal belongings were packed in wooden chests.

Most important, the Pilgrims needed enough food and drink for everyone througout the voyage—although they didn't know exactly how long that would take. They brought meat and fish that had been salted, smoked, or dried so it wouldn't spoil. There were no refrigerators at the time. They also brought pickled eggs, cheese, and crackers called hardtack. To drink, there was beer and wine.

FOOD AND DRINK

Fish, and meat that was salted, smoked, and dried

Vegetables such as onions, cabbages, peas, turnips, and parsnips

butter, cheese, hardtack (crackers)

oatmeal, flour, dried peas, dried fruit

Vinegar, mustard seed, oil, spices

Beer and wine

PROVISIONS FOR USE ON BOARD THE SHIP AND UPON ARRIVAL

candles, soap, firewood

pots and pans, crockery

clothes, bedding, and tablecloths

Books, including bibles, almanacs, and hornbooks for the children

The Pilgrims also had to think very carefully about what they would need for their brand-new settlement in America. They knew that they would find wood in the forests for building houses, and that there were animals to hunt for food. But they had to bring everything else.

Animals

A passenger named John Goodman brought his two dogs on the Mayflower—a spaniel and a large mastiff. There were probably also small farm animals, such as pigs and chickens.

GOODS TO TRADE WITH THE NATIVE AMERICANS

Beads and jewelry

cloth

Mirrors

Knives

TO USE ON ARRIVAL

All manner of household goods and furniture (including mattresses made of coarse cloth and filled with straw)

Looms and spinning wheels to make cloth

Tools for building houses, farming, and fishing

seeds and grain to plant in the fields

Weapons such as guns and knives, and even cannons

John Alden

Much of the food and drink was stored in barrels, which were taken care of by the ship's cooper, John Alden. He had the important job of making sure the barrels were kept in good condition so that the food would be safe to eat.

A Stormy Journey

The voyage seemed to go on and on, as the Mayflower pitched wildly in the choppy waves. The stormy sea sometimes made it too dangerous to light lanterns, or to light a fire for cooking—or even to go above deck to empty out the smelly chamber pots over the side of the ship.

The Pilgrims tried to keep their spirits up. They sang and they prayed. They tried to ignore the sailors who mocked them when they were seasick. One sailor was especially cruel with his taunts. By a twist of fate, this sailor was the first of two people to die during the voyage. His body was thrown overboard.

During one particularly violent storm, a huge wave slammed against the ship, cracking a large wooden beam. The captain, Master Jones, didn't know how to repair it. But among the tools the Pilgrims had brought to build their new settlement was a device used to lift heavy objects such as the beam. It worked! The ship's carpenter then secured the beam to a post to keep it upright and the *Mayflower* continued on.

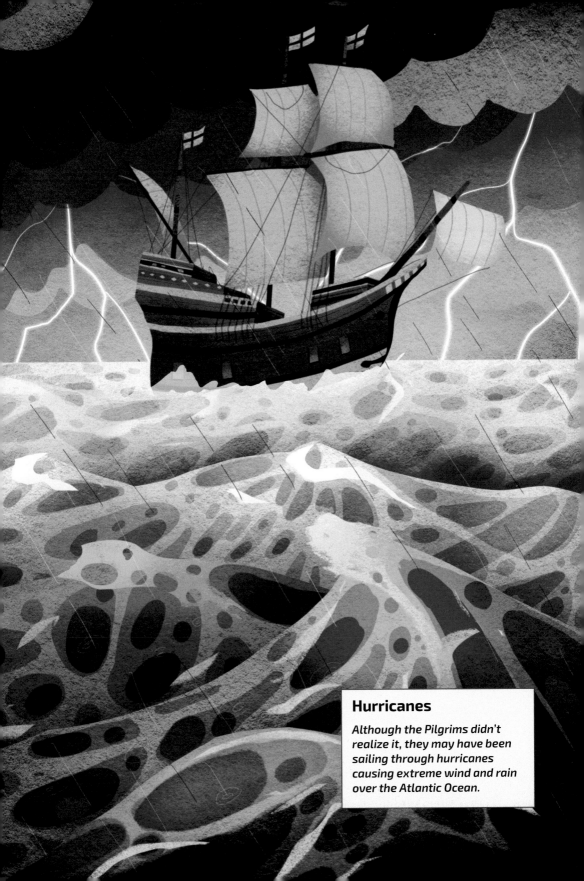

Hurricanes

Although the Pilgrims didn't realize it, they may have been sailing through hurricanes causing extreme wind and rain over the Atlantic Ocean.

Man Overboard!

One day, a servant named John Howland was desperate for some fresh air. Despite yet another storm raging around the Mayflower, he climbed up from the 'tween deck to the top deck.

But on the top deck, he had trouble keeping his balance as the waves thrashed the ship this way and that. Poor John Howland stumbled to the ship's rail and fell overboard!

Earlier, Master Jones had decided that the storm was too strong and he had rolled up the sails, leaving a section of rope called a halyard dangling in the sea. Now, as John Howland struggled to remain afloat in the violently churning sea, he managed to grab hold of the halyard and clung to it for his life. Luckily, he was young and strong and able to hold on to the rope until the crew threw him a boat hook and pulled him back on board the ship. It was a close call.

The Howlands

John Howland and his wife, Elizabeth, went on to have ten children and 88 grandchildren! There are now about 2 million people who are descended from John Howland. They include actors, writers, Olympic medalists, and even United States presidents.

George H. W. Bush

George W. Bush

Land Ahoy!

At sunrise on November 9, 1620, the passengers on the Mayflower were woken by excited sailors. They pointed to sandy dunes in the distance. Land at last! Imagine the Pilgrims' joy and relief after 66 days at sea.

But according to Master Jones's calculations, they had arrived at Cape Cod, an arm of land reaching off the coast of what is now the state of Massachusetts. This was about 200 miles (320 kilometers) north of the mouth of the Hudson River, where the Pilgrims were due to establish their settlement.

Master Jones turned the *Mayflower* southward toward their destination. Soon, they found themselves sailing through dangerous churning waters that were too shallow for the ship. Would the *Mayflower*'s voyage end here, smashed against the rocks on the coast of North America?

Cape Cod

The Pilgrims were not the first to spot the dunes of Cape Cod. Captain John Smith of Jamestown fame had named it Cape James, after the English king. In 1602, Bartholomew Gosnold, another English explorer, gave it the name Cape Cod because of the abundance of codfish there.

⇩ Mayflower in Plymouth Harbor by William Halsall.

Finally, by midafternoon, the tide rose enough for the ship to continue sailing. But it was too much of a risk to sail south toward the mouth of the Hudson River, so the *Mayflower* headed back up north, to Cape Cod.

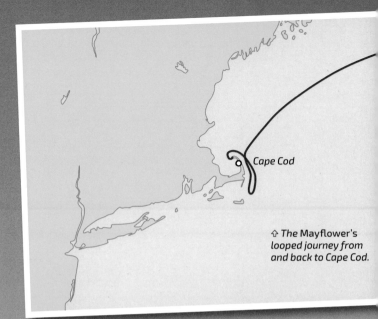

Cape Cod

⇧ The Mayflower's looped journey from and back to Cape Cod.

William Bradford

". . . after [a] long beating at sea, [we] came to that land, which is named Cape Cod."

The Mayflower Compact

If the Mayflower landed on Cape Cod instead of its intended destination, would the rules of the original contract still apply? Would the new settlement dissolve into lawlessness and disorder?

The Pilgrims decided to draw up a new agreement and continue to work together for the good of the settlement. Whether they had started the journey as Separatists or Strangers didn't matter.

⇧ The original document has disappeared, but William Bradford rewrote it for his book Of Plymouth Plantation.

On the morning of November 11, 1620, with the *Mayflower* anchored off the coast of Cape Cod, 41 men signed the agreement that became known as the Mayflower Compact. Their first elected governor was John Carver.

Although the Mayflower Compact is famous for giving power to the people, it didn't give power to women. It would be another 300 years before women had the right to vote in the United States.

Governor Carver

John Carver had been one of the organizers of the venture to America, and he was well respected by the other Pilgrims, who elected him governor of their new settlement. Sadly, Carver died suddenly in April 1621. William Bradford replaced him as governor.

⇦ 41 men in total signed the Mayflower Compact.

One of the key terms of the agreement was that the people would elect officials to govern the new settlement. Having come from Europe, which was largely ruled by kings and queens, this concept of democracy was a new—and a very important—idea. Another important idea was that the new settlement would have a civil government that was separate from the church. This gave the Pilgrims freedom to choose their own religion.

Scouting for a Home

Two days later, the eager passengers were finally ready to disembark. Master Jones anchored the Mayflower in the large harbor at the end of Cape Cod, and the crew ferried the Pilgrims to shore in rowboats.

Imagine walking on land after more than two months at sea, with fresh air and wide open spaces after the cramped, smelly 'tween deck of the ship!

But the land around the harbor was sandy and not suitable for farming. A group of men led by Myles Standish used a boat to scout around for a good location for the settlement. Would they meet some of the Native Americans that they had heard about?

Myles Standish

Captain Myles Standish was the Pilgrims' military chief. He was an English soldier who had become friends with the Separatists while stationed in Holland. He sailed on the Mayflower with his wife, Rose. Standish was small but tough. His nickname was "Captaine Shrimpe."

In fact, they did spot some Native Americans in the distance. The scouting party looted things from the Native American huts and dug up their graves. Perhaps they left beads or something in exchange for the things they took. Or perhaps, like many Europeans exploring the New World, they simply did not respect the fact that Native Americans already lived there.

In any case, the angry Native Americans responded by shooting arrows at the Pilgrims, who fired their muskets in return. Thankfully, no one was injured on either side.

Eventful expeditions

During their three expeditions, the scouting party lost their way and got stuck in the snow. William Bradford even found himself dangling upside down from a deer trap in a tree!

Settling in Plymouth

Meanwhile, a new baby was born on board the Mayflower *while it was anchored in the harbor. Susannah White named her little boy Peregrine, which means "pilgrim." But there was tragedy, too.*

William Bradford returned from one expedition to discover that his wife, Dorothy, had drowned. Some thought she missed her son back in Holland so much that she threw herself into the freezing cold water.

It was cold and damp on board the *Mayflower*. Many of the the Pilgrims became ill, and some died while waiting for the scouting expedition to return.

Pilgrim houses

The Pilgrims used tree trunks stuck together with clay to build their houses. It was a common building technique in England called "wattle and daub." The roofs were thatched with reeds.

You can visit a reconstruction of the Pilgrims' settlement called Plimoth Plantation. The old spelling of Plymouth was "Plimoth."

It was mid-December by the time the Pilgrims chose the site for their settlement. There were streams full of fish and fresh water, and a large rock on the coast that became known as Plymouth Rock. There were even fields that had already been cleared. The Pilgrims got to work building their settlement, paying little attention to the human bones and skulls that they found scattered around the area. They called their settlement Plymouth, after the town in England where they had sailed from.

Plymouth Rock

Legend has it that the Pilgrims landed at Plymouth Rock, but there is no record of this. It is not mentioned in William Bradford's Of Plymouth Plantation.

Disease strikes

But that winter, disease spread quickly. Within a couple of months there were only about fifty Pilgrims left—fewer than half the number who had set sail on the Mayflower.

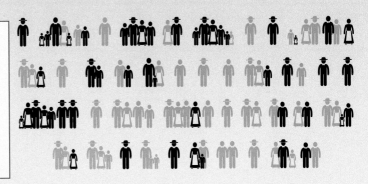

Wampanoag People

The land where the Pilgrims built their settlement had been a Native American village called Patuxet, belonging to the Wampanoag people. Wampanoag means "People of the First Light."

For about 12,000 years before any Europeans arrived, tens of thousands of Wampanoag people had lived across the region that is now known as the states of Massachusetts and Rhode Island. Then sadly a plague, probably brought by Europeans, devastated the population between 1616 and 1618. The Wampanoag deserted the village of Patuxet, leaving behind the bones and skulls found by the Pilgrims.

⇩ Everyone in a Wampanoag family helped gather food, which was roasted over the fire or grilled on hot stones.

"Kwe!"

The Wampanoag were generally peaceful people. They lived in dome-shaped huts like the ones that the scouting party had looted on their expeditions. They grew corn, beans, and squash—staple crops known as the Three Sisters. They hunted in the vast forests and fished in the rivers and streams.

Massasoit was the Wampanoag leader. In fact, his name meant "great leader." Massasoit didn't trust the Pilgrims. Previous Europeans had not only spread disease but were also known to kidnap Native Americans and take them across the ocean. What would these new arrivals do?

Wampanoag words

kwe (KWAY)—hello

sachem (SAY-chum)—leader

wetu (WEE-too)—home

mishoon (mih-SHOON)—canoe

waban (WAY-ban)—wind

wunniook (wuh-NEE-uck)—be well

Unexpected Welcome

One day in February, a Pilgrim out hunting ducks on the marsh spotted a group of Native Americans. He hid in the long reeds until they were out of sight. Then he ran back to Plymouth to warn everyone.

Other Pilgrims noticed smoke rising into the sky, mysteriously missing tools, and two Native Americans standing on a nearby hill watching the Pilgrims. Captain Myles Standish wasn't taking chances. He had cannons moved from the *Mayflower* to a hill where they could defend the settlement.

About a month later, a Native American man approached Plymouth. He had long black hair and wore a leather strap around his waist. He walked toward them, confidently and without fear. The Pilgrims watched in astonishment, curious children standing wide-eyed in doorways as he passed their houses.

Distrustful Pilgrim men stood in his way to stop him from going farther.

But the Native American man came to greet them. "Welcome," he said.

This was Samoset. Imagine the Pilgrims' relief at meeting a friendly native who spoke their language.

⇧ Samoset visited Plymouth and spoke to the Pilgrims in their own language

Samoset's visit

Samoset was leader of a tribe farther north, and he had learned a little English from some fishermen there. He enjoyed the food and drink that the Pilgrims offered him, and he spent the night as a guest of the Hopkins family.

Cape Cod

● Plymouth

Wampanoag

The Peace Treaty

Samoset told the Pilgrims how they had settled on land abandoned because of disease. He also told them about Massasoit, the great Wampanoag leader. The Pilgrims invited Samoset back to Plymouth with some of Massosoit's men to trade goods.

On one visit to Plymouth, Samoset introduced the Pilgrims to Squanto (also known as Tisquantum), a Wampanoag man who spoke fluent English. Squanto would become vital to the Pilgrims' survival in Plymouth. One of his first tasks was to interpret during a meeting between the Pilgrims and Massasoit, who had traveled to Plymouth to see them.

⇩ *Squanto taught the Pilgrims how to plant corn, as well as fertilization techniques.*

It was an occasion of great ceremony. Massasoit arrived flanked by sixty Wampanoag warriors. (The Pilgrims only had twenty men.)

First, Edward Winslow presented him with gifts on behalf of the Pilgrims. Captain Standish led Massasoit to meet Governor Carver, who was accompanied by a small parade led by a drummer and a trumpeter. Then, with Squanto as interpreter, the two leaders worked out the peace treaty that united the Pilgrims and Wampanoags as friends and allies.

⇨ Squanto also helped the Pilgrims on business matters—translating and showing them how to trade with the Native Americans.

Helping each other

The Pilgrims needed the Wampanoags to teach them how to survive in the New World. Although Massasoit didn't trust the Pilgrims at first, the Wampanoag population had declined recently, so he needed the Pilgrims as allies to show power to other native tribes.

Squanto

Squanto was a native Wampanoag from the village of Patuxet. He had been kidnapped by English explorers and taken to Spain to be sold into slavery. He escaped to England and joined a ship sailing to North America, but on arriving home, he found that most of Patuxet had been wiped out by disease. Squanto then helped Englishman Thomas Dermer trade with Native Americans, before returning to the Wampanoags.

Thanksgiving

That spring, Squanto and other Wampanoag people taught the Pilgrims vital skills for survival in the New World. They taught them how to plant kernels of corn, showed them how to catch schools of fish that filled the brook, and demonstrated how to fertilize the cornfields with fish manure.

⇩ Together, the Pilgrims and Wampanoag celebrated for three days.

Changes

In April 1621, John Carver died suddenly and William Bradford became the new governor of Plymouth. Katherine Carver died soon after her husband, leaving only four adult women out of the eighteen who had sailed over on the Mayflower.

On April 5, 1621, Master Jones and his crew set sail on the *Mayflower* to return to England. The Pilgrims all chose to remain in Plymouth, where they were now committed to making their home. John Alden and some of the other crew members also stayed.

By the fall, the Pilgrims had grown a small crop of corn, wheat, and other grains. They decided to hold a feast to give thanks for their harvest. They feasted on wild turkeys, ducks, geese, eels, fish, and shellfish, plus nuts and berries, and dishes made with the grains that they had grown. Massasoit arrived with about ninety Wampanoag people—almost twice the number of Pilgrims left in Plymouth. They brought five freshly killed deer to add to the feast.

Thanksgiving

Harvest festivals had been celebrated for centuries in both the European and Native American cultures, but the legendary feast of 1621 is considered the first Thanksgiving in the United States. Thanksgiving has been an official annual holiday across the country since 1863.

Plymouth Grows

About a year after the Mayflower had landed, another ship arrived in the harbor. The Fortune had sailed from England with 35 passengers, including the Brewsters' eldest son. Robert Cushman, who had organized the Pilgrims' journey, was also on board.

During the next few years, more ships arrived, with many families being reunited. There were soon weddings to celebrate, and more children were born. The settlement grew. By 1627, around 160 people lived in Plymouth.

The Pilgrims were very busy working the fields, hunting, and fishing. They also built new houses. The children worked hard, too. They gathered firewood, fetched water, ground corn, fed livestock, collected eggs from the hens, and milked the goats. There was no school, but some children had lessons at home. They probably enjoyed games that modern children still play, such as leapfrog, hide-and-seek, checkers, and tic-tac-toe.

Repaying the debt

Robert Cushman told the Pilgrims that the investors in England were demanding to be repaid as soon as possible, so the Pilgrims loaded the Fortune with wood and furs and other American goods for the investors. The Pilgrims would continue repaying their debt for several years to come.

Pilgrim Talk

Good morrow—hello
How do you fare?—How are you?
Huzzah!—Congratulations!
Fare thee well—Goodbye
Perchance—maybe

"Huzzah!"

"Perchance I shall win . . . yes!"

War

Decades passed and more settlers arrived, mainly from England. Some joined the Pilgrims in the village of Plymouth, while others started new settlements in the area. Some original Pilgrims also moved out to other settlements. They wanted more land for their farms.

Although the peace treaty with Massasoit and the Wampanoag still held, competition for land caused tensions between settlers and Native Americans. Tensions also grew among different Native American tribes in the region.

William Bradford looked on the changes with sadness. The Pilgrims' aim of establishing a small settlement for the purpose of religious freedom had instead turned into a pursuit of land and wealth. Bradford died in 1657.

⇩ *Nearly 8 percent of men who lived in the Plymouth Colony died during King Philip's war.*

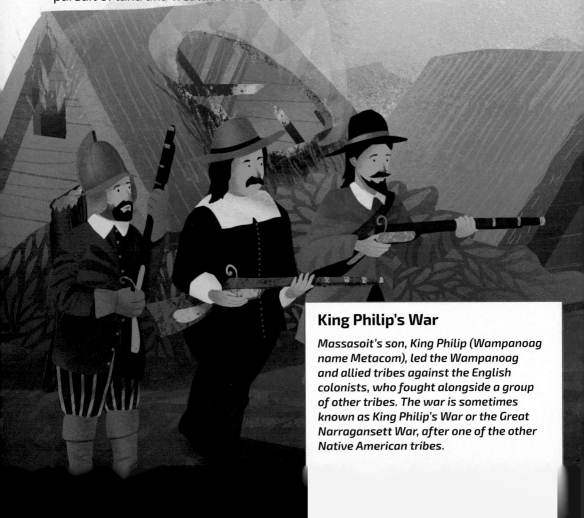

King Philip's War

Massasoit's son, King Philip (Wampanoag name Metacom), led the Wampanoag and allied tribes against the English colonists, who fought alongside a group of other tribes. The war is sometimes known as King Philip's War or the Great Narragansett War, after one of the other Native American tribes.

In 1661, Massasoit died. The colonists became more demanding. They cleared whole forests where the Native Americans hunted in order to make way for their own farmland.

The conflict erupted into a fierce and bloody war in 1675. It marked the end of the peace. After that, white settlers across North America regularly attacked Native Americans and took their land.

First People

Indigenous people such as Native Americans are also called "First People," because they lived on their land for thousands of years before colonists arrived from Europe. Indigenous people now make up less than 5 percent of the world's population, spread across about 90 countries. Many of them are still struggling for their rights.

North America

Canada

Inuit people lived in the cold Arctic north of Canada, while Native American tribes lived in the south. Then French explorers Jacques Cartier, Samuel de Champlain, and others arrived in Canada during the 16th and 17th Centuries, and a mix of French, English, and Scottish colonists settled there.

Africa

Latin America

Many native American tribes lived in Mexico, Central America, and South America before explorers arrived from Spain and Portugal. Spanish explorer Hernando Cortes and his army conquered the native Aztec Empire in Mexico in 1521. Spanish and Portuguese settlers spread throughout the region.

South America

Siberia, Russia

Several groups of indigenous people live in the Arctic region of Russia known as Siberia, including Inuits. The first Russians settled in Siberia in the late 16th Century, and most of the rest of the region came under Russian rule in the 17th and 18th Centuries.

Europe

Africa

Many indigenous people live all across Africa. Between the 16th and 19th Centuries, European slave traders transported millions of indigenous African people to slavery in the Americas. European settlers also colonised various places across Africa, taking land from indigenous people, like the Xhosa in South Africa

New Zealand

Maori people were already living in New Zealand when Dutch explorer Abel Tasman recorded the first sighting in 1642. In 1769, James Cook claimed New Zealand for the British. During the same voyage, he also claimed Australia.

Australia

Australia

Aboriginal people had been living in Australia for about 50,000 years before explorer Captain James Cook claimed it for Great Britain in 1770. Among the first settlers in Australia were prisoners who were shipped from Great Britain.

The American Melting Pot

An immigrant is someone who settles in a new land. The Pilgrims were among the first immigrants to the New World.

With the exception of Native Americans, everyone who lives in the United States is descended from immigrants or is an immigrant themselves. Many immigrants have arrived since the Pilgrims, and more are still arriving. They all make up the enormous melting pot of people who have come from all over the world to make their homes in the United States.

⇧ *Young European immigrants arriving on Ellis Island in 1921.*

The Statue of Liberty

The Statue of Liberty, which was given to the United States by France, opened in 1886 to welcome immigrants to the country. The famous poem on the pedestal of the statue reads:

*"Give me your tired, your poor,
Your huddled masses yearning to breathe free,
The wretched refuse of your teeming shore.
Send these, the homeless, tempest-tost to me,
I lift my lamp beside the golden door!"*

—Emma Lazarus

⇧ *European immigrant children arriving on Ellis Island in 1921.*

Ellis Island

Today, almost half of all Americans are descended from immigrants who arrived at Ellis Island in New York Harbor. Between 1892 and 1954, more than 12 million immigrants arrived there by ship. At Ellis Island, the immigrants waited for many hours in long lines. First, they had medical inspections. Then they were interviewed by immigration officers.

Some immigrants already had family or friends in the United States, but others were alone. Like the Pilgrims, they all had to learn a new way of life in their new country. Often, they had to learn a new language, too. It wasn't easy, but they were determined to make a new home, not just for themselves, but for future generations.

⇧ Immigrants could convert their money to American dollars for no charge.

⇧ The first sight that greeted new arrivals was the Statue of Liberty.

The Immigration Debate

These days, there are a variety of reasons why people move to different countries. Some move for jobs or for a different lifestyle. Others move to be with someone they love. Still others move to escape danger.

Some people think immigrants should be allowed to move to any country they choose. Remember, the Pilgrims came from England and then moved to Holland, and then to America. Shouldn't we all be able to find homes where we can be happy and safe, even if it's not in the country where we were born? Besides, it's fun to share each other's cultures—and food! The world is changing and everyone is mixing together.

⇩ *St. Patrick's Day is celebrated around the world on March 17*

⇩ *Women in San Antonio, Texas, carry an altar in the traditional procession for the Day of the Dead (Día de los Muertos) celebrations.*

Other people argue that those who are already citizens of a country should have first dibs on things such as jobs, homes, and schools for their children. They don't want more immigrants because they're afraid there won't be enough for everyone. They also don't want the traditional culture of their country changing to include immigrant cultures.

What do you think about the immigration debate?

European Union

The European Union (EU) is a group of 28 countries (as of 2018) in Europe. People who are citizens of those countries can choose to immigrate to any country within the EU.

⇧ Chinese New Year celebrations in Canada

Refugees

Sadly, some people must escape their home countries to seek safety elsewhere. These people are refugees.

According to the United Nations, a refugee is "someone who has been forced to flee his or her country because of persecution, war, or violence." (Persecution is cruel treatment "for reasons of race, religion, nationality, political opinion, or membership in a particular social group.") The Pilgrims were persecuted in England because of their religion, and they became refugees who found safety in Holland. Another word for safety is "asylum."

Kindertransport

The heroes of Kindertransport rescued about 10,000 children from Nazi-occupied countries between 1938 and 1940. They brought the refugee children to safety in Great Britain. The children most likely would have died otherwise.

Today's Refugees

The United Nations estimates that every day, 44,400 people are forced to flee their homes and become refugees. About 2.6 million people currently live in refugee camps. These camps are meant to provide temporary accommodation, but many refugees stay for years because they have nowhere else to go.

Imagine being a refugee today and having to leave your home country to find safety somewhere else. After what might be a dangerous journey, you finally arrive at the border of a safe country. Will they let you in? That is the problem faced by refugees.

Do you think countries have a responsibility to accept refugees? In 1948, the United Nations Declaration of Human Rights set out basic rights for all human beings around the world. Included are the right to a safe place to live and the right to find a safe home in another country.

⇦ *These refugees are escaping danger in their home countries. They want to live in a country where they can be safe.*

Research Your Family

How did your family come to be in the country you live in now? Ask your parents, grandparents, and other relatives what they know about your family history. Are there people in your family who have come from other countries? Find out where they're from. Look up the countries on a globe or map.

Maybe you're an immigrant who has left one country for another. Or maybe you have friends who are immigrants. Look up their countries and mark them on a globe or a map.

The Author's Family Immigration Story

You could mark your family's immigration on a map like this:

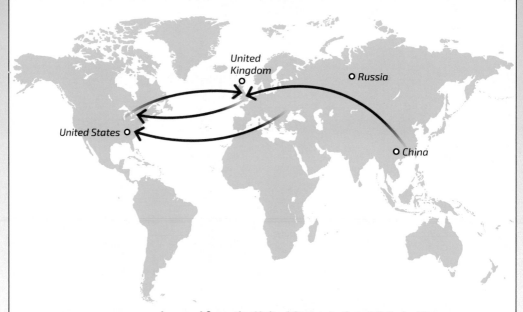

Note that throughout history, countries change names or their borders move, so finding the exact countries can be difficult.

I moved from the United States to Great Britain. Many years before, my grandfather moved the opposite way—from Great Britain to the United States, where he arrived at Ellis Island. Going back further, several of my great-grandparents immigrated to the United States from Russia and countries in eastern Europe. A few years ago, we added another country to our family immigration story when we adopted our daughter from China and brought her to live in Great Britain.

These are other people with immigration stories:

⇦ Olympic gold medal runner Mo Farah immigrated to Great Britain from Somalia as a child. Mo had to work hard to learn English. Some of his family moved to Great Britain with him, but the rest, including his twin brother, stayed in Somalia.

⇧ President of the United States Donald Trump has an interesting immigration story. His mother came from Scotland, while his grandfather on his father's side immigrated to the United States from Germany. His wife, First Lady Melania Trump, comes from Slovenia.

⇨ Sergey Brin is one of the founders of Internet search engine Google (which also owns YouTube). As a child, he immigrated to the United States from Russia.

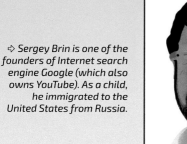

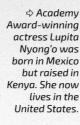

⇨ Academy Award-winning actress Lupita Nyong'o was born in Mexico but raised in Kenya. She now lives in the United States.

⇦ Sisters Yusra and Sara Mardini were among a group of refugees fleeing war in Syria on a boat in 2015. When the boat nearly sank, they jumped into the sea and pushed it safely to shore. Yusra and Sara now live in Germany. Yusra is an Olympic swimmer and a Goodwill Ambassador for the United Nations.

Glossary

Asylum Protection given to people who are fleeing their home country because it is not safe for them to live there.

Belief Something that a person considers to be true, and influences the way they live their lives.

Catholic A member of the Roman Catholic Church.

Colony A place set up and ruled by people sent from another country. English colonies set up by the English settlers were ruled by England.

Cooper A person who repairs and makes wooden barrels and tubs.

Democracy A system where people are able to choose, or elect, how they are ruled and governed. For the Pilgrims, a democracy replaced a monarchy, which is when a royal family rules.

Descendant A person related to someone who lived long ago.

Government A group of elected officials who decide how a country or territory is run.

Immigration When people move from one country to another to live. A person who immigrates to another country is called an immigrant.

Melting pot A place where people of lots of different ethnicities, cultures, religions, and identities live and work together.

Native Americans People or descendants of people who originally lived in the Americas. Native Americans lived on the North and South American continents before immigrants chose to settle there.

Pilgrim A person who makes a journey, specifically a religious one. The people who travelled on the *Mayflower* to the New World are known as the Pilgrims.

Pilgrimage The journey made by a pilgrim is called a pilgrimage. Many people go on pilgrimages to religious sites and holy places each year.

Protestant A member of a Christian church that separated from the Roman Catholic Church in the 16th century. The Church of England was one of these churches. King Henry VIII was a protestant.

Puritan A Christian in 16th and 17th century England who disagreed with some of the Church of England's practices.

Refugee A person who has been forced to leave their country to escape war, violence, or persecution, which means being treated cruelly because of their race, religion, nationality, political opinion, or membership of a particular social group.

Religion A system of rules and beliefs that guides some people in living their lives. Many religions involve worshiping a god or multiple gods.

Separatists In the time of the *Mayflower*, a person who wanted to separate from the Church of England and worship in their own way. Many Separatists had to leave England to worship freely.

Settlement A place where people set up a new community, build their houses, and establish their new way of life.

Strangers The people who journeyed on the *Mayflower* that were not Separatists. The Separatists called them Strangers because they didn't know them before traveling together.

Treaty An agreement made between two or more countries, states, or people who govern an area. The Pilgrims made an agreement with Wampanoags to be friends and allies.

Index